DATING *IS* A GAMBLE

DATING *IS A* GAMBLE

Dating When The Stakes Matter Most

BY: ANTHONY DRAYTON

© 2019 By Anthony Drayton

ISBN-13: 9781693751516

Printed in the United States of America

TABLE OF CONTENTS

ACKNOWLEDGEMENTS

First off I would like to give thanks to me number corner woman my mother that has stuck with me throughout this boxing career I call life. Without her I never would have made.

I want to give thanks to my family members that are no longer here my grandmother and my stepfather that have given me so much knowledge throughout this journey to get to this point and place right here

Wanted to give a special thanks to these 2 gentlemen for helping me out along the way. Juvone Geigher for tell me that I needed to put my ideas down on paper and make it into a book and Robert Lewis help me out in the 4th quarter with coming up with more ideas.

Given a lot of praise to all of the family and friends that said at my panel and gave their ideas their experiences and their knowledge on all the toppings put in front of them.

I have to give acknowledgement to all of the women that I've dealt with over the years to come up with all that this material that is put forth in front of you the reader.

I have to give thanks to the person that helped me put this project together Geo Derice.

Last but not least I would like to give a thanks to myself for having the courage and the confidence to join the great world of authors to actually put idea to paper.

INTRODUCTION

N ot another one!

Yes I know what you're thinking, another dating book? C'mon son! This is like beating a dead horse. Every single day it seems someone is talking about relationships. It's a hot topic and the tabloids always cover them, but is it really necessary to have another dating book out in the market?

My simple answer is yes, but I'll explain why.

For over the past 10 years I've recalled the many of conversations that has been centered around relationships with my guys. I'm talking about the conversations that often never gets recorded, does not get remembered, and is often never repeated out loud. These are unfiltered conversations that come from the mouths of men when it comes to their experiences with women. Wouldn't you want to be a fly on the for those conversations? Imagine being able to realize that the stuff you are thinking about others have been thinking about it too? What if someone went through what you are about to go through, what would that feel like if you could get some information ahead of time to avoid fall in the pot holes of relationships. No one wants to be stuck in relationships they had no business being a part of, but how come men find themselves in these situations so often?

This book is an attempt to finally pull back the curtains and share the bar conversations at Applebees while the Knicks are breaking my heart yet again. Could you imagine if men were as faithful to their women as they were to the beloved Knicks? The Knicks can lose by 50 points to a crappy team and a man will say that's my team with a sense of pride that would make you think it was 1979 again, the year the Knicks won the championship.

As I reflected on the many conversations I've been a part of, the advice that I've received and also given to men, I realize there is so much information out there that sounds good, but in practice really make no sense or have deemed to be ineffective. What if someone can really tell it like it is, without finding a way to make it sound good or clean, but just get to the root and tell how to really play the game of finding the right mate.

Now if you've been reading this far into this introduction you're probably the type of person I wrote this book for, but before I tap into that I want to give those who are not a fit for the book a chance to get off the bus right now. You see if you are the person who thinks they know everything, you have no issues, you can do no wrong and you not going to change anything, then the journey can stop right here. You do not have to proceed reading further because there will be stuff in this book that will challenge you to change your ways. For the men, this book is not about how to be a player. By player here is what I mean. You've ever seen someone say they play ball, but then they get on the court and you can tell that was just lip service? Like real talk, they are a disgrace to the game of basketball and watching them play is as painful as hearing someone scratch a chalkboard? If that is you this book is not for you. However, if you are the type that has had their share of dating episodes and now cannot afford to go ahead and get it wrong or want to improve your odds on playing a winning hand for the long haul, this book is my gift to you. Women if you're reading this, you know how they say women are from venus and men are from mars or is it men are from venus and women are from mars, you get what I'm saying LOL, this book is for you because you will get an understanding of how men think.

Men view dating when done seriously like gambling. It's risky business. When gambling for real not for fun, you don't play the game the same way. You need strategy, you need to do whatever it takes to increase the odds of winning, you are selective, precise, you understand the rules, you know how to break the rules, you just a wealth of knowledge all around. This book is a guide that will provide that knowledge of how to date when the stakes matter most. You'll learn when to play, how to play, why you have not been playing the right way before and so much more. That's all in the first section of the book. The next part we will be diving into when to fold. You see every hand you get is not the hand you should stay with. There are times when you just have to fold and that is a good thing. Many relationships fail because people don't know when to fold. Holding onto something that is failing and going to ultimately fall apart is like holding onto a hot frying pan, the longer you hold it, the more it hurts. In this section it's not only about when to fold but the best practices on how. If you want to avoid songs like I bust the window of your car, you are going to want to dive into this section and learn how to fold with grace so that girl does not mess up your space (house, car, whatever you like). The last part of this book is what I call "ALL-IN". This is when you have done your due diligence, played the game well, have overcome the obstacles that could have folded your relationship and now are ready to take things to the next level.

The stage has been set, you know what to expect moving forward from this book. It's going to be real, rough, and rugged, but also will help produce results. I wish this information was a conversation when I was growing up and coming into the game. I wish someone would have showed me how to play, but I was not privilege to that information. It's said that wisdom is learning from the mistakes of others and boy have I made some mistakes. I grew up around a ton of women and had few of any men to show me what to do and not to do. It's my hope that you will not have to make the mistakes I made, that you would be wise to pick up this book, read it, and talk about it with other men. Women do it all the time, that's why they better at dating than we are TYPICALLY (every group of people have their exceptions). You're holding in your hand a guide that desires to close the gap. These are the conversations we should be having, the thoughts that should be shared that will help us get to where we ultimately want to end up and that's with a winning hand and the lady of your dreams.

And one more thing before we jump into the first section of this book. The reason I really wanted to write this book is because I realize that our lives when broken down can be traced by to our decisions. When we make the wrong ones, our lives reflect that. Many homes are broken because of the decisions that were made or the decisions we fail to make. Many broken hearts could have been avoided, perhaps many domestic disputes, and divorces could have been prevented had real conversations taken place about how to date when it matters, when to play, how to fold and when to go all-in.

The excuses are gone now, this book is that conversation, the playbook is in your hands, so let's get to the first step and start playing.

Section I:

When To Play

CHAPTER 1:

WHY PEOPLE AREN'T PLAYING

This opening section of the book we will be tackling "When To Play".

This section is specifically for those who are tired of playing in scrimmages where the stakes do not matter. It's like looking at a pre-season basketball game, no one ever cares what the scores are of those games. When the stakes matter though, when the wins and losses count that is when people want to take things seriously and this is what this section is all about and designed to do. If you are not ready to find miss right or go on the path towards it, this section is not specifically for you, although I would encourage you to read it so that you know what is ahead of you when you are done playing around. I'll even pull back the curtains and explain why us men do not like to sit at the playing table when the stakes matter and share strategies and tips that can help you build the confidence you need to turn the odds in your favor. I know relationships can be scary especially to men because it's not something we grew up studying or talking about. It's my hope this section of the book will help to ease that anxiety a bit, get you feeling a little bit more in the know and help you finally win more at serious dating.

Before knowing how to play, it's important to breakdown the reasons why men don't play or don't want to play when the stakes matter. It's almost as if they are afraid, kind of like a basketball player who refuses to take the final shot. I will say this later, but scared money don't make no money, so we are going to tackle this fear head on. Playing not to lose is not an option here. Winning is the only option as Eminem said, failure is not.

We are going to dive into the 3 major reasons why men do not join the game when it comes to serious dating in this chapter.

Reason 1: Too many choices

Have you ever been to Cheesecake factory? If you have then you know it is probably the last place you want to take someone who is indecisive because the menu there has so many options. You can get all kinds of stuff on it. Likewise when you don't see a man want to commit the reason has a lot to do with the menu of women that is available. I guess you can say God was too good at creating because of the all types of women that are out there. There is tall, short, thick, skinny, all different races, vast personalities and so much more. It's no wonder why there is a culture where men just have a hard time to commit. It's as if the mindset of a man is, "I cannot just have one", because they are all good. For men they want to create a dream team, when many women dream of prince charming (one guy) and that is it. I cannot think of a guy growing up saying I'm looking for my Cinderella or Belle from Beauty and the Beast.

The issue when it comes to having too many choices is the fact that you have a hard time making a choice at all, which makes dating seriously a great challenge. You can turn the corner and find 3 of the same type of women and all 3 of them have one or two things that make them unique and all over again us men are stuck at what to do when we are faced with those situations.

I compare it to going to a restaurant and they telling you all the different options you can have with the order you're making. And unfortunately for men, when we hear options, they are not looked at as optional, instead they are looked as a test where there is a,b,c,d, and all of the above. Men like the all of the above option.

The negative thing when you want all the choices is that some of the choices might not be the best and this is where men can fall into the trap of thinking many is a good thing. That would be like having 10 bench players instead of having 1 superstar on your team. Would you rather have 1 Michael Jordan or would you like to have 10 Bill Wenningtons and that is no disrespect to Bill, but you get my drift.

Quantity is not always the best, when it comes to dating quality is what the goal should be but that is not necessarily the case for men. What makes this hard for men to navigate is the fact there is no filter that they've been taught. Think about doing some online shopping on nba.com website and you know you only want knicks gear. This is something you can easily filter and eliminate other options but when it comes to filter the choices of women, what criteria are men exposed to? Typically these are limited to physical features only, which we will discuss later on within the book. It's important that you have a gameplan so that you can narrow down the list of options that are available. This is the only way you will be able to make a sound judgment on the playing table and place a bet that has a higher likelihood of succeeding.

To ensure that this is no longer the case we have a serious of questions that men should have in their mind to help with the filtering process. These questions are just guides but are great for helping narrow the amount of choices that are available.

Filter Question: What do you want?

This question is important and is a great filter. If you want a girl that does not smoke, that cuts off all the girls that do, already narrowing down the options. If you want a woman that is into physical fitness, than that narrows down the options even further. It's important that you know what you want or you might just end up with someone that you do not want. Men are notorious for skipping this step only to regret the relationships they got themselves into for skipping this. Take this as a warning, do not skip this step. A little extra time spent ahead figuring out what you want will save you months, or even years of down the line headaches. Trust me, I've been through this myself and know first hand what compromising what you want or not knowing what you want can lead you to losing it all.

Another great question is…

Filter Question: What don't you want?

A great example of this is if you were going to go to a car dealership and you mention that you don't want a front wheel drive car because you want something you can drive all year long, no matter what the weather is. This is another tool that can help filter out options so that it is easier to make a decision or to at least have only a pool of options that cater to what your want and needs are versus just having too many choices to choose from.

These two questions will help you go a long way, but I must share something with you that I wish someone would have told me. Do not solely focus on just your wants, focus also on what it is you need. A wise person once said to me, "what you want might not be what you need and what you need might not be what you want." Be aware that making decisions on just wants might get you in trouble, men especially because they typically want things that fade such as looks. The girl with the beautiful body is the one I want, but is that girl full of themselves, high maintenance, and more of a headache then you would like or too much for you to handle? These are things that men need to have conversations around more, which is why I am mentioning it here. No longer is the excuse of I did not know applicable. That's the excuse I would use time and time again until someone informed me. Now I am informing you.

After talking a ton of guys as I was surveying them for this book I realize that while too many choices is definitely one of the reasons why they are not ready to sit at the table and play for real the game of serious dating, it's not one of the top 2 reasons why they won't.

Reason 2: Men Are Scared

Don't hate me fellas. I know we are king kong, macho man, the incredible hulk and all the avengers combined when it comes to our toughness but real talk, if we are keeping it a buck (100) we are scared of what playing the game actually means. When it comes to fear, a lot of times it's about us being afraid of what we do not know. There is a fear of the unknown that plays a big role. Men like to provide answers to problems, but they are not fond of having a ton of questions. Questions such as what will they be able to do or not do, questions such as does this girl want me for me or is she setting me up to change me to who she wants me to be, these questions are all legitimate in the minds of men and gives cause for pause when it comes to being a serious relationship. Take for example men popping the big question of "will you marry me"? This is a scary thought for a lot of men because this means it's very serious the relationship, it also gets us thinking what change will my life go through as a result of this decision. What does saying "I do", really mean? Does it mean I don't get to do XYZ anymore, and we not talking about the fact you cannot talk to other women any more but also the idea of can you hang out with your boys like you used to. Change is a part of the journey that is inevitable but not all change is bad and that is something men have to learn.

Another part of being scared or having fear is the acronym False Evidence Appearing Real (F.E.A.R.). In the mind of a man there is a reality that they think will take place that they are fearful of. This could sometimes be comparable to how kids feel about a monster under their bed. If they think there is a monster under their bed it's just as good as there really being one. I don't mean to call men a bunch of kids but real talk we can be sometimes and that story that may not be true can cause there to be a halt in proceeding in a serious relationship.

While this all is understandable though, is the idea of possible losing out on Miss Right a worthy one? That is for each man to ask himself and see what their answer is. Many people miss out on life's best opportunities because of fear or being scared and that is no difference here.

As they say, "scared money don't make no money". The same can be said about relationships, if you are scared to come to the playing table, then you won't get a chance to take part in being in a serious meaningful relationship.

Reason 3: Men Expect To Fail

This one is closely related to the fear/scared part but this is more so generational. For many men they have not had the opportunity to see many successful relationships or successful marriages. Some studies show that almost 50 percent of marriages in the United States alone ends in a divorce. That alone would make a person not find success at the playing table.

Those are not favorable odds that would make you want to take a risk like putting up your chips and going all in on someone. This is where men would rather go with reason 1 and say I rather not put all my eggs in one basket just in case things do not workout. What is interesting though is when you expect to fail, the odds of failing increase.

Take for example a game we used to play growing up called "punch buggy". For those who might not know what the game is, you punch the arm of the person you are playing with when you see a Volkswagen Bettle of a particular color that you stated. The minute you put that out there all of the sudden you find the very thing you are looking for. It's the same when it comes to relationships, if you are looking for the relationship to fail, you will find it. The best piece of advice is to think positive and expect it to work, but evidence in a lot of upbringings for men does not support this kind of thinking.

When you combine all these three reasons together you can see that the cards are stacked up against the likelihood of men feeling like playing the serious dating game is a safe bet or a bet worth taking. It would take a very special lady to go ahead and break pass all these potholes that prevent men from experiencing a smooth ride on the road of love. These reasons while valid do not have to stop you from experiencing love. Many men are single today and do not have the help mate designed for them because they let the idea of picking one stop them or they are scared and fearful that things won't work out or the fact they are not guaranteed that it will workout at all.

This is why we call dating a gamble. You don't know 100% for sure what the result is going to be, but it is still possible to know how play a lot better so that you can find success despite what your past may teach you.

CHAPTER 2:

THE COMMON POTHOLES

Fool me once, shame on you; fool me twice, shame on me.

Have you ever been in a situation where you got something wrong because you just did not know? Ever get into trouble because you did not know the lay of the land or have an idea of the mistakes you were making. When it comes to playing the game of dating when the stakes matter, there are common mistakes that men make that prevent them from placing winning bets at the playing table of love. When I mention common, the funny thing is that these mistakes are not common to the man though. It's like the saying, "common sense isn't so common", that applies here as well.

Many times if you knew where you would mess up the fool me twice part would never come to be, but because you did not know, you could not grow up and make better sound decisions. It's almost as if just like driving there are blind spots that we as men have when it comes to dating that opens up the door for making costly mistakes when it comes to playing the love game. After reading this chapter though you no longer will have that issue as I breakdown the common mistakes that men are not aware of or not consciously aware of. When you know better, you can do better, so let's dive into knowing better by talking about the common errors of our ways.

Common Mistake #1: Inability to read signs

Imagine this. You travel to a foreign country, let's take Canada for example and you see the signs which are obviously written in french, what is the likelihood if you cannot read the signs that you will be able to get to your destination safely? The odds would be slim to none right? Maybe perhaps you might get lucky but can you imagine driving and not being able to read the signs? That driving experience I'm sure will be a frustrating one. For many men driving down the road of love is a frustrating one as well and a big part of why is because of our inability to read the signs well. You've heard me mention this before but it's worth repeating again, most men have not been exposed to what serious dating is like. They are not use to the dating when the stakes matter, so because of it they often do find themselves fooled once, twice, maybe three or four times even. They then go ahead and believe that it was not meant for them to do this well and become players for life. This does not have to be the case, you just got to know what the signs are. The ability to read signs in a relationship comes from repetition. There is a saying that says, "repetition is the mother of all learning". Your inability to read the signs in a relationship is not because you are not smart, but instead has more to do with your exposure. It's like reading. The first time you read something it was not that easy, but as you saw the words over and over again they got easier. It's the same thing with this. You will read the signs better the more you're exposed to it. Now I'm not saying that you need to go date the whole playboy mansion to learn how to do this, you can learn from the mistakes and experiences of others.

For example, if you see a lady asking you to buy a bunch of stuff for her right out the gate in a relationship, that might be a hint that she is a gold digger or someone who is only with you for the things you can buy for her and not really into you. Many times as men we overlook this sign because we think about things with just our eyes. We not only don't read the signs, sometimes we can go ahead and ignore them outright. I can go real deep on this topic, but that's reserve for another chapter, but know that sometimes paying attention actually pays dividends in your relationships. Not paying attention though is the most expensive bet and risky bet you can make.

A simple way to help you read the signs better is to actually care more about what is happening. Question what you see happening instead of just going for the proverbial "joy ride". Don't just go buy a bunch of stuff for the lady, maybe ask what you like about this, why does this matter to you. The asking of the questions will help focus you and the person you're with. The questions will help to make sure you do not live out common mistake number two!

Common Mistake #2: Living in a false reality

Do you know what a mirage is?

No I'm not talking about the hotel in Las Vegas, although it's funny we are talking about betting, dating when the stakes matter, and talking about a mirage.

A mirage is something that appears real or possible but is not in fact so.

Another way to define the word mirage is an optical illusion. When searching for a synonym for the word mirage things such as fantasy, hallucination, and trick come up. Unfortunately many of us get into relationships that is all fantasy and no reality. We fall into the trick of what it looks like and never realize what it really is. This is a result of not being able to read signs, ignoring the signs, or wanting something so bad that you make up what it is even though it's not.

It's hard to have something real if all you see it through is fake. There's a quote that says, "Avoidance is the best short-term strategy to escape conflict, and the best long-term strategy to ensure suffering." When I first read that quote it cut me at my core and more so because it's so true. Many people don't want no problems in their relationships, so we say stuff like "it's not that serious" or "ain't nobody got time for that" and then what happens is yes we do escape the conflict for a little while but long term what happens? We suffer. We end up in relationships we should never be in or deplete all our resources, our chips on a bet that quite frankly was not worth it.

Every now and then when you in a relationship do a REALITY CHECK. These are quick short conversations where you ask real questions so you can make sure you are not living in a mirage, false reality world. Take the temperature of the room figuratively speaking. Ask the other person on a scale of 1 to 10 how are you feeling about this relationship, what can be improved upon, what should I stop doing, what should I start doing. All of these questions will snap you our of this false reality. It's almost like someone who has been put under a spell. Love can do that to people in relationships and sometimes we do not realize it until it's too late. It's like the casino giving you a bunch of drinks so you do not realize how much money you really losing or the weight of the decisions you're making. Do not fall into this trap or make this mistake.

Remember you might get fooled once, but getting fooled twice, that's on you.

Common Mistake #3: Focusing On What Matters Versus What Doesn't Matter

Albert Einstein once had a quote that said, "Not everything counts can be counted and not everything that can be counted counts." At first glance this quote can make your head hurt trying to figure out what this really means, but after seeing it broken down it makes perfect sense. Allow me to illustrate this. Let's take for example a basketball player like Draymond Green of the Golden State Warriors. What is counted in basketball are stats, such as point per game, rebounds, assists, steals, blocks, turnovers, things like that. On the surface Draymond Green's points per game might not be anything to write home about, maybe statistically he does not qualify to be one of the best players in the NBA, however the Warriors know that his value is not by what is counted, but more so the things that cannot be counted such as passion, energy, effort, hustle, attitude, things like this is what makes him so great.

When it comes to relationships, we can make the mistake many make with sport athletes in just focusing on what can be counted. An example of this might be a woman's bra size, how big her butt is, her weight, her height, how much she got in the bank, just to name a few. On the other hand while this might be important from a preference stand point is that what makes a relationship work? Is a big butt what makes a relationship work or is it the mindset of the person? No one wants a big booty negative nancy in their lives but one of the mistakes is focusing on only what can be counted. It's important that if you are going to play this game right to focus on what matters versus what doesn't matter. This is an area where you have to really look deep within yourself to determine what your deal breakers are. What are the must haves, what are the needs that you have for the other person? At the end it is those things that ultimately determine whether it's a safe bet to put your chips up.

Mistakes are bound to happen. They are inevitable. By no means do I want you to have a fear of failing so much so that you are not willing to play the game unless you are guaranteed a win. That's not living. Those who live are the ones who are willing to lose, which also makes the door open to win a possibility as well. By knowing the common potholes that you will find when you are looking to win the game of love when the stakes matter most, you will know how to play much better, decrease the odds of failing, and thus have a better experience, increasing your odds of winning and actually be glad about the decision you made to play in the first place.

Now I know there will be some people who read these mistakes and think they do not do it or that they are easily overlooked. I too felt the same way until a failed relationship showed me otherwise. My goal in writing this is to lessen the chance of you having to experience a failed relationship because sometimes that failed bet can be too costly. Many men are fathers of children they wish they never had because they got into relationships they never should have been a part of. This happens more so than I'd like to admit and that is because information like what is shared in this book is not common. Because it's not common, the mistakes like the ones listed above are easily repeated. It's like that saying, "if you do not know your history, you are bound to repeat it", if you do not know the common mistakes or the common potholes, you are bound to drive into them. If you're not careful you might drive into a pothole that you nor your car can survive, so be careful, do not be stubborn, open your mind to what was shared and be sure to share it with another so a new history can be created.

CHAPTER 3:

ARE YOU READY TO PLAY?

I was born ready.

This is typically the answer you hear when some-one is asked, "Are you ready?".

I hate to admit this but many times in my life I've done things where people asked me "Are you ready", and I answered by saying "I was born ready", but in reality I was not. There is this idea that if I think or say something then it automatically is. I believe this thought came from the time period where the law of attraction became super popular from the movie "The Secret".

Many times we think that just by thinking something it is, and while that can be a step in the right direction, it is not the entire staircase. It's important that when you are going into something that you do your due diligence. There is a verse in the Bible that speaks on this very well.

"For which of you, desiring to build a tower, does not first sit down and count the cost, whether he has enough to complete it?" - Luke 14:28

By no means am I getting spiritual on you but this verse speaks a ton of facts. In our case we are not building a tower, but if someone was to call their relationship a tower, that's not a bad look. A tower is a tall building, something that is of great height. Who wouldn't want a relationship that is of great heights, something that everyone can see, model, be inspired by? We all would sign up for that, but it's not as simple as just thinking it. It requires deep thought. Cal Newport, a popular author would call it "Deep Work". There are levels to this. It's not as simple as just saying I want it or having cute sayings like "I was born ready". You're really ready when you look deep into things, sitting down and evaluating thoroughly what it is you have, is it worth betting your chips knowing there is a risk that you can lose it all? It might be best to say that the safest bet is one that you analyze and look at from all the possible angles that you can before jumping in. Now as a word of caution there is no guarantee that even after taking a deeper look that something won't go wrong. This is not a step meant to show you how to make sure nothing goes wrong, but it's irresponsible to not take a deeper look first before moving forward to minimize what wrong can happen.

Take for instance you are buying are a car. Would you take the salesman at their word if you asked, "is the car good to go?" and the person responded, "the car is born good to go"? Chances are you would want the Carfax, you want to take the car for a test drive, see the what the features are and so on. The same applies to when you are deciding if you are ready to play this game for real, for real.

A deeper look isn't just limited to you looking at the other person too. It actually has a lot to do with the deeper look within yourself. Are you ready for what this means? Are you willing to deal with someone who might want or need something from you? Are you over your past hurts from previous relationships? Is there any unresolved issues that have gone unaddressed? These are all questions you need to ask and ask of the one you're looking to date before you move forward.

A deeper look also is making decisions not just off your emotions. A recent study by a Harvard professor showed that 95% of purchasing decisions are subconscious and that is heavily ruled by our emotions. Emotions play a huge role when it comes to making decisions and the behaviors we have when it comes to buying stuff. A relationship is like a purchase, you're buying into the idea of being with one person or committing to one person. Making a bet is a decision. Have you ever made a decision you regretted? If you were to diagnose that decision how much of that decision was rooted in emotions versus being rational? I bet it would be close to the percentages that the Harvard professor came up with. Emotions are great in getting people to get off the couch and do something, but sometimes minus some rationale can lead to a whole heap of trouble. Emotions are heavily tied to feelings, and feelings are fickle and need the support of something else in order to help in fostering the best decisions. Where should that support come from?

Your brain. Your brain is able to process things and should be involved in the process of deciding if you are ready to play and the other decisions that come down the line such as should I stay in the relationship or not, is this relationship one that I should go all-in on or not. These are all decisions that you need to sit down and count the cost of. Counting the costs just with your emotions are not enough in my opinion. You need backup and the brain is that backup that you need. When you use your brain you can be more confident or more assured about the result of the decision you're making.

What does this look like practically? It's seeing a woman that got a banging body that you are excited about being with (emotions), but asking the question with your brain is this woman what I need or does she have the things you need to have success long term in the relationship. Emotions will make the decision for you now, the brain makes the decision for the later. It's important that if you are going to be in a serious long term relationship that now and later is accounted for. Often men are all about the right now. It's why we rarely have an answer for the question, what's your five year plan? When it comes to finally playing the game right with the goal of finding that person to build your life with, these questions are not only relevant, they are necessary.

With all that being said, are you ready to play? That is a question you need to ask and you need to ask it with both your brain and emotions in mind, preferably with your brain first. The brain will set the foundation, a solid one that your emotions can then build off. The scrimmage is over, the regular season is here. What is at stake now matters and knowing how to play it well is crucial. We've broken down the common mistakes, we discussed the reasons why men have a hard time playing or why they are reluctant to play the serious dating game. The reality? It's not our fault that we have failed to find success when it comes to serious dating. The information was in a vault and not accessible, the mindsets needed to win have never been uncovered. But now we know more, we know better, and can do better as a result. You now know to read the signs, you know how to walk in what is happening really and not a mirage. You know now what matters and the things that don't. You know now that what you want is important but not as important as what it is you need. A new history gentlemen can be created with this new found knowledge. Go out there play the game, step up to the betting table with your chips in hand. In the next section we will be discussing what do you do when you are at the playing table itself. What happens when you are dealt a hand and do not know if you should play it or fold. We will discuss the idea of quitting and whether it's all bad or are there moments where it helps us versus hurting us. I'm excited to share this section because if you thought the mistakes we discussed were bad, the stakes are a lot higher when you're in the middle of the game. It's like making a turnover in the opening quarter versus making that same turnover in the 3rd or 4th quarter. The stakes are higher and that means we got to bring a higher version of ourselves to the table. Fasten your seat belts, here we go.

SECTION II:
WHEN TO FOLD

CHAPTER 4:

WHY MEN DON'T FOLD

"Quitting is not giving up, it's choosing to focus your attention on something more important."

Do you agree with the quote above? For men especially we hear things such as never give up, winners never quit and quitters never win, all sayings that tell us all the reasons to stay in things even if those things might not be producing anything positive for us. I know this can be odd to talk about when to walk away from the betting table in a book that is convincing men or showing men how best to play at the table. It's important to know when it's best to go and step away from the betting table as well. Many relationships go from bad to worse because of sayings like "never give up" or "quitters never win and winners never quit". These statements have some truth to them and it's not a flat out false statement but there are times when quitting is a good thing. You've heard of the saying quit while you're ahead right?

Let's take for example you came to the betting table with $20 and you gamble it and end up with $1000. You just made 50x the money you originally came to the table with. Now some people might say, hey you got the midas touch or the lucky hand so keep on playing because that $1000 can become $50000, but at the same time you can also end up losing it all too, a risk that just might be too risky to take. Sometimes you want to be happy you won, and in relationship all it takes really is just one major win. Relationships is the gamble of a lifetime and when you win it, there is no need to try your luck over and over again. With that being said however why is it that men find themselves in relationships that they got no business being in. This is specifically for the men who are serious about dating, the ones who ae still players this does not apply to you, but when you want to go ahead and make the relationship work, you are ready to settle down, it's important you know the moments where folding makes sense, which is one step before deciding the ultimate step of going all in, which we discuss in the next section of the book.

I've uncovered that there are 3 things specifically that prevent men from folding. These 3 things very well might be the reason for abusive relationships, divorces, fatherless homes, and so much more. I believe that things get worst instead of better because of the mentality of never folding. Sometimes it's best to walk away from things and some relationships are not worth the risk or bet of staying in it.

Number 1: Men Are Too Confident

Listen when it comes to getting a lady, being confident is a good thing. In fact ask any woman if they would date a man that was not confident and you will get a result of zero. Confidence is attractive, confidence or swag, that is a turn on for many. When you have confidence it can give off the impression that you have self-love and self-respect, which makes it easier for you to be able to give that love and respect to someone else. However, too much confidence might make you play a hand you had no business playing because you think that everything can work, that you are invincible and cannot be stopped. This kind of thinking is naive and really can turn you from someone who is playing the game to getting played.

Too much confidence shows up when men think that what they have or the power they have is so strong that it can overcome any obstacles or defeat all the odds. This is a nice mindset to have but the question I would ask you the reader is if your confidence is rooted in reality or is it rooted in a mirage. Too much of anything is not a good thing and too much confidence is no different.

Number 2: Pride

Closely related to being too confident is the idea of pride. When you have pride, you do not want no L's on your record so you stick it out, you work on the relationship, you try to fix it, you manufacture success, or you play it off like it's all good, when it really is not. Pride will blind you and immediately have creating a mirage of your relationship. Someone with too much pride is bound to get humbled at some point.

Perhaps pride is the reason why some athletes never win a championship. They decide to go down with the boat. Take for example Russell Westbrook. Pride might be the reason he won't leave Oklahoma City Thunder or pride might be the reason why instead of playing a style of basketball that will help change the team's playoffs misfortunes that he continues to play the game the way he does. By the way I'm a huge

Westbrook fan so by no means am I hating on him, but it's important for you reading this to be willing to put your pride aside, to swallow your pride for the bigger cause, a ring, a championship or for the sake of this book, a relationship worth going all-in.

Number 3: Men love to conquer

Tell a man what he cannot do and he will get all his ducks in a row to conquer that thing. Men love a challenge. It's why playing hard to get works so well for women. A men will chase you, we by nature are hunters. The issue though is when we hunt blindly. We hunt to protect our pride, our ego, and end up making decisions solely off of emotions and not using like mentioned in the previous part of the book, our brains.

Not everything you want is worth conquering. You have to choose your battles. I know we like to win, but sometimes a lost today can help create a win for the future. In the NBA the Sixers would call it "trusting the process", while others call it tanking. If you are tanking with a plan or there is a purpose behind it, don't frown against doing it.

The worst thing that can happen is you conquering something that will one day conquer you or overthrow you. I rather get rid of the thing that can down the line be the root of my demise.

In addition to this there is a mindset that a lot of times people have when faced with tough situations. I remember when I first learned of the term , "stockholm syndrome". Stockholm syndrome is defined as a condition that causes hostages a psychological alliance with their captors as a survival strategy during captivity. Back in 1973 is when this term was first used in the media when a bank robbery was happening in Stockholm, Sweden. Hostages refused to testify in court against their captors even though they were released. Sometimes we can be hostages in our own relationships and become so loyal to the thing or one that has us in captivity. This might feed your never quit attitude or your pride, but it's only going to leave you bitter and broke.

The men that fall victim to this condition are more so the ones who have low self-esteem and believe they cannot get anyone better. They are typically with the women that others would consider to be the trophy wife. Because the woman is a prize, they automatically believe it justifies the torture that they are enduring. While there are sacrifices to be made in a relationship, we must always take a moment to evaluate what is happening and ask ourselves is this still worth the bet I'm making. This question can save your pockets, keep you from getting into altercations because your bitterness got out of hand and so much more.

This is all blueprints, footprints, roadmaps, that I wish I heard when I was dating or before I got married. It's like the quote Steve Jobs said, "you cannot connect the dots going forward, but you always can going backwards". Looking back I'm noticing how the mistakes or thought patterns that I've grown up with play major roles in the decisions I've made and the ones I failed to make.

As I said before, you can only do better when you KNOW better. Raise a glass in the air to knowing better and doing what we know.

CHAPTER 5:

WHEN TO FOLD

"Quit while you are ahead, all gamblers do". Dating is the ultimate gamble. There is no certainty and there are no risks. In the last chapter we discussed the reasons why men don't fold, walk away from the table. In this chapter will map out exact situations where it makes sense for you to walk away from the table. Sometimes the best thing you can do is leave a situation instead of staying in it. Imagine you were on a plane and you heard that it was going to crash, you wouldn't stay on the plane right? You would hope that you paid attention to the instructions in the beginning of the flight and grab your yellow vest, pull on the tubes and jump the heck out of that plane. The last thing you want to do is be like the people who stayed on the boat in the Titanic movie and ended up dying.

I'm going to share with you the situations where it makes complete sense to fold your hand and not bother playing any further. These situations are often things that can go undetected or us men have a hard time explaining. Women are so good at voicing why things are not working, but us men are not the best at reading signs or being present to realize what is happening or how to vocalize it so your partner would understand. It's why communication is so key in relationship and a skill we as men should work to develop and get better at.

One situation that it makes sense to fold is when there is disrespect in your relationship. For men respect is very big. In fact there is a great book called "Love and Respect" by Dr. Emerson Eggerichs where he talks specifically about how men desperately need respect and women most desire love. Respect is how men receive love or interpret love. When a woman disrespect you, men interpret that to mean they are not loved by the woman. I remember a friend of mine who is married sharing with me an example in the book where a woman would go make a decision about the relationship or household but did not consult with the man. The man got real upset about it, more so than the woman could ever understand. You see the man felt like there was a level of disrespect that something involving them was not brought to his attention. This is not so much about control, but more so to do with courtesy and making him feel that he is a part of the relationship. A man will step up their love for a woman when the woman respects him.

If you are in a relationship where you feel disrespected be sure to express that but after a while is that woman is just not going to respect you or belittle you because you might not have something that is on her checklist such as a college degree that's a red flag and reason to leave. Sometimes a woman will disrespect you because of your level of education or where you came from. Perhaps it can be as simple as them not consulting you with things they think require high intellect because you did not finish college or have just a GED. This judgment is something that can be toxic in a relationship, highly disrespect and lead to problems down the line that you want no part of. When watching television shows that showcase domestic issues or when a man goes outside his relationship, it's often a respect issue at the forefront, especially if they meant to be in the relationship they were in.

Another situation when you want to fold is if you are in a relationship with a negative nancy. This is someone who is always looking at the glass half empty. This kind of mindset is not one you can build anything with. You want someone who is positive, optimistic but keeps it real, and gives you good vibes. A negative person is one that just is not compatible with you. When dating you normally do not pick this up out the gate because everyone tries to make a good impression in the beginning. As you dig deeper or are in the relationship longer, truer colors come out and you get to see the person for who they are. In a relationship of sometime you get to face some adversity or some pressure. They say pressure can bust pipes or make diamonds. How does the one you dating respond to adversity or pressure. If they are always going negative you do not want to try to build something with that person. Do you have dreams and your significant other is always pointing out why it cannot work or won't work? This is a sign they may be a negative nancy. Now by no means am I saying to have a "yes" person who cannot tell you the truth. That would be basically a false reality or mirage and that as we discussed earlier will not help your relationship. However you want someone who you do get good vibes with, where you feel supported. Remember this is going to be the person you are possibly doing life with, so you want to think about what it would be like to have this person by your side. If you know this person is not supportive and always negative it's a good idea to fold your hand

and step away from the betting table. That's a bet NOT worth making.

The last scenario mentioning is being in a relationship that simply is too much for you to handle. Now again this is something most men won't admit. That superman complex makes us think that we can handle everything, fix everything, only to realize too late that you cannot handle it all. This is why it's imperative to not let your pride or ego win out because you will not fold, stay on the playing table and lose your shirt, and everything else that you own. It's okay to walk away and say that this bet is just too costly, that I cannot handle it right now, that I do not know how to handle that. Being a superhero or macho man is not a reality that you want to face. Those characters are fictional that you see on television, this is real life. Sometimes folding means taking a pause and other times it's a clean break up too. Either way you want to go ahead and act. Staying in this kitchen will get you burned. Be honest with yourself and if it's too much, say so. It might even save your relationship doing so or might free you from being in a relationship you should not be a part of.

Speaking of folding and knowing why men don't fold and when it's best to fold, it's important that I share with you the best ways to fold. Not all folding is created equal. There are some break ups or pauses that can cause some serious unrepairable damage. The next chapter we'll talk about what are the best steps to folding. I even consulted a few ladies to get more insights on best practices for folding. This is the kind of folding that will ensure that while the relationship is dead, you won't have to be.

CHAPTER 6:

BEST WAYS TO FOLD

I got a bet I want to make with you.

I'll give you $100 if you can tell me in the next 3 seconds who is Neil Sedaka.

1...2...3... Times up. I'm pretty sure you have no idea who he is. Neil Sadaka was a singing who in 1962 came out with the song "Breaking Up Is Hard To Do". This entire section we talked about why is breaking up hard for men, when it's best to break up (fold) and now we are entering the chapter where we will talk about the best ways to break up. You did know there is a bad way to break up right? Bad break ups can be flat out deadly.

Some of the most famous black movies such as "The Brothers", "A Thin Line Between Love and Hate" all depict the struggle that comes with breaking up or moving on in a relationship. In the movie "The Brothers" one of the ladies can be seen shooting up a house because her man did not want to be with her anymore and was going to call off a wedding. Guys take that as a clue, folding when you got as far as planning a wedding is not a good look. That is a clear example of you did not speak up earlier or was not keeping it a buck with the person you were with to wait all the way to that point.

How can we forget about "A Thin Line Between Love and Hate", one of Martin Lawrence classics.

This is a good movie that shows what happens when folding is done incorrectly. At one point the Martin Lawrence character Darnell views the Brandi played by Lynn Whitfield as the prey, the thing that he wants and then it turns on him as things get out of hand and he becomes the prey and Brandi becomes the predator, but the one that Darnell needed really was Mia played by Regina King and not Brandi. This is a great example of need versus wants and what happens when folding is not done right. Grant it Brandi was a little crazy it shows later on in the movie, but often times this happens when folding is not straight forward, or when you do not notice the signs that would tell you this might not be what I need.

The longer you stay in the game the more the other person becomes a dealer who won't let you out of the game. It's almost like joining a gang, the longer you in it, the more stuff you know, the more involved you are and the less likely you are going to be able to get out. In fact the longer you stay, the more costly or expensive its s to get out. This is the same when it comes to dating. Now there are times where folding can happen too soon but we will tackle that at the end of this chapter.

As far as the best practices for folding, the key is being straight forward. It's said that the quickest way from point A to point B is a straight line. This too, should be the case when it comes to folding. It should be quick, not long and drawn out. You do not want to beat around the bush. I got a call while writing this book with a few ladies that I know and asked them the same question about folding. I asked them specifically what is the best way for a man to fold, one that would not get your windows busted or have them wanting to key your car or shoot up your home. The consensus was to be straight forward and honest. They mentioned that it hurts more when you beat around the bush and lead them on than it would if you were to just hurt them right then and there and move on. Going through the motions, making believe y'all good does no good to you or the other person. The hesitation to keep it a buck is that you will feel compelled to stick around in the relationship longer than you should. That is when you start justifying why you cannot fold by saying stuff such as "look how much energy and time I put into this relationship, I gotta make it work." Gotta make it work is not a good position to be in. That means that you are operating out of obligation and not operating from a place of joy or excitement or something that you want.

Another thing when folding is do not do it over a text message. I know it's 2019 and modern technology is a beautiful thing but folding is tough as it is and the same way you would want the respect to have someone tell it to your face and not duck and hide, the same courtesy should be extended to someone you were in a serious relationship with. I know that it's easy to break someone hurt over a phone call or over text message, but it does not offer closure for real and it probably isn't the approach that someone would respect. Even with saying this I know that many of you are rolling your eyes, throwing your hands up in the air and saying I cannot believe you asking me to do this in person. You'll be proud that you did because like we talked about earlier, that is something a woman at the very least can respect you for doing.

So how to fold best? Get straight into it. Do not beat around the bush, be honest. A recommendation is to use the criticism sandwich. Have you heard of this? A criticism sandwich is when you put the negative statement in between two positive statements. The negative is the meat and the positive is the bread. This helps to make things end on a upswing. Now I will be honest some people might not receive the sandwich well, but this has been proven in many circles to work very well when you are dealing someone bad news, such as you're firing someone, which you are doing in a relationship when you are folding.

Before moving forward to the final section of this book, the "Go All-In" section, it's important for you to know that there is such a thing as folding too soon and I would be doing a disservice if I did not bring that up here. Sometimes we can misjudge or be quick to judge things. We can misread a situation as well. Sometimes you can misread a situation as well. This reminds me of the talk shows on television back in the days where you would say this girl or guy is wack and then a few years later you see that glow up and start saying to yourself, I had her, she was mine and had I stayed just a bit longer this would have worked out for me. I'm not telling you to right at the first sign of trouble, but I am saying to be aware and make sure the moment does not become a monument that just does not go away. I remember seeing this scenario play out in Tyler Perry's movie, "Acrimony". The character played by Taraji P. Henson named Melinda who was there for her man Robert played by Lyriq Bent. She decides to call it off after folding and then gets upset when she sees that another woman by the name of Diana played by Crystle Stewart is the one that is benefiting from the things that she believed she could have had if she stayed in the relationship. Now many will say that she did not fold too soon, that he was taking too long, but that is the risk that is made when you do fold. The person might not have been who or what you thought. Grace is necessary for the race towards finding love so be mindful to not just throw in the towel so fast. However, if what we discussed in this section repeats itself then you owe it to yourself to not be insane. Insanity is doing the same thing over and over again expecting a different result and that is not something I wish for you to be or experience.

That puts a bow on this section. The last but not least section is the one that you've been waiting for. How and when do we go all-in. When do you put all your chips up and say I'm going for it. This section won't be the longest, but it's the one that we all hope to experience one day. That is my hope for you.

Section III:
When To Go All-In

CHAPTER 7:

GOING ALL-IN

I t's time to take off the seat belt.

We've reached the part of the book that I've been building up towards from the introduction. The time where you finally take all your chips and push it to the middle of the table. We've discussed when to play, why you don't play, folding and the best practices to doing it and now we have finally reached the point of going all in. This is a big stage for men because quite frankly it's not our nature to get to this point culturally. Culture says the man is the one who can get many girls, but this is a different kind of man we are talking to. We are talking to the man who is focused, looking to take things to the next level. We are talking to the man who is done with the pre-season games and practices and is ready for the holy grail, the super bowl, going for the championship. It's my hope that this book thus far has been a reminder in some regards and also at the same time brought up things that has never been a conversation amongst men before. This is the book that I wish I had when I was coming up in the game. I made practically every mistake you can make and it's the reason why I've been able to compile the wisdom that comes from the experiences that I've been through and now sharing it with you.

When it comes to going all-in this is the stage where you have done all your research. This is the time where you've asked the questions you needed to know and not just going off your wants. You've done the work to find out all there is about the person you're with. Here are signs that you are ready for this stage.

- You have a 3-D look of the person you are with.
What I mean by a 3-D look is that you not only have
your point of view of the person, you got the point of
view from multiple sources. You know what your friends
thinks about the person, your family has met the person
and has shared their thoughts. You've met with the family and friends of the person to get an idea of what she is
like with her friends and family. You've seen her in different habitats, at work, at home, on vacation, at family
dinners, and know what makes her laugh but also what
makes her cry. You are not looking at this from just one
angle, but you have explored all the angles.

- You have asked the tough questions. Tough questions are not easy to ask but if you want to get far you
have to ask them. Questions like have you ever been
sexually assaulted? This is a tough question to ask but
it is an important one to know because it can impact
long term the intimacy or lack thereof in a relationship.
A warning though with the tough questions. When I in-
terviewed some ladies these questions did ruffle some

feathers. It's best to ask these questions later on in the relationship. Ladies did not have an issue answering this question after 12 months. They also mentioned that a question like that should not be asked without the conversation of a future with them. Due to how personal in nature the questions can be it is important that you use wisdom and proper judgment to know when exactly is best to ask these questions. Timing is important, but do not let that stop you from asking because knowing the answer to these questions are important as well.

- You're aware of the strengths and weaknesses of the person. You know how to best approach these things and know when to be patient and when to push to help build the person to the best version they can be and the same applies to you. There is a trust that both parties are in it for the right reasons and are FOR one another. This is important if you are ever going to become one in marriage. You must be on the same team.

- You know their past history. It's not important for you to know everything but it is important for you to know the important things. History has a weird way of repeating itself especially when it goes unaddressed. Knowing the history allows you to know how best to navigate the present so you can build towards a future together. In this you want to get the information you need to know and not fight for petty information that is just gossip or irrelevant. Focus here on what matters the most. Something like you have a child in a previous relationship or that you were once married, that is something that would matter. A sign of what matters is information that can impact something in your future. A child or a marriage from your past definitely can play a role in how things go in the future and is why it's important to have this information.

Once you are well researched, you can go ahead and proceed and be confident with the bet you are making. It's different when you sit on the betting table and fully understand the rules of the game, the tricks of the trade, and know how to get in and out of various scenarios as we discussed in this book.

The last thing I want to leave you with before putting a bow on this book is share with you what makes a good hand. These are the 5 cards that you need to know 100% for sure that you are ready to go all-in. Think of these cards like a royal flush.

Card #1 - Compatibility

We define this as having shared values. This is where you have things common and say the world through the same lens. Compatibility shows up in many different areas such as spiritual, financial, mental, physical, religion, family dynamics, lifestyle and personalities. When how you feel in these areas are alike with your significant other you are heading down the right path towards making a bet with great odds. Sometimes you won't find perfect synergy in these areas. At times you might have slight differences but as long as they are complimentary they can work. The last thing you want is to not be on the same page or the both of you are reading a completely different book altogether. No need to go all-in if that's the case because the bet won't be a worthwhile one for the long term.

Card #2 - Communication

This is a captain obvious one but no relationship can exist without communication. Communication is rooted in being truthful and honest. It's living in the reality. It's being able to use your words and be understood while also understanding the other person. If you feel like you do not care enough to listen to your girl then it's a red flag that you just might not be ready for the all-in stage. However effective communication is a two-way street. She listening to you, and you listening to her. There's no couple that can survive a lack of communication and but there is very little that can break a couple up that has strong communication.

Card #3 - Assistance/Support

You know what it's like when someone does not support you? What are the odds you're going to want to love this person or give that support back. You want to make sure you are supportive of the other person and that person is supportive of you. Blind support is not what we are talking about here. You want to be positive, cheer the other person on, be their mirror and give them occasional reality checks like we talked about earlier in the book. In this case two heads is better than one, so you want to make sure that there is a culture of support from both of you.

Card #4 - Serenity (Sense of Peace)

Calm, cool and collected. That is what you are looking for in your relationship. There is a saying that says, "when you love what you do it does not feel like work." This is a goal you want to have for your relationship. When you love the person to the point where it does not FEEL like work, you're in a good space. There should be a calm, coolness to your relationship where you know what you are going to get. You not looking to be predictable but you want to be confident in what it is you have.

Card #5 - Stability & Growth

Last but not least, stability and growth. You never want to get someone who is going to stay the way they are. If you date someone and they are already at the mountain top, then there is only one direction left to go and that is down. You want to be with someone who is growing and that growth cannot happening with a stable foundation. Buildings cannot be built without a foundation and neither can a relationship work without stability. What are you confident in about your relationship? Can you trust the person to do what they say they would? Are they all talk but no action or do what they say match what it is they do. Note that the girl will be looking for this from you and so should you.

When you have these 5 cards in play, you got a hand that is worth playing and going all-in with. These things make up a foundation that is worth risking all your chips for. Communication, compatibility, stability/growth, a sense of serenity or peace and that support are key ingredients to a winning recipe.

CONCLUSION:

Wow! You've made it. Did you know that many people start a book and never finish it? If you survey men who read a book about dating, the odds are even smaller. I hope you got some good information, good reminders that you can implement and be aware of for your next shot at serious dating.

Dating is the ultimate gamble. Anything that involves another person, where emotions such as love is present you're looking at some risky business. However information is key to minimize the risk. When you know better, you can do better. This book is a compilation of all that I know. Of course it won't be my last book and nor will it be the last book on relationship written by a man for men. It's a start. It's a beginning to getting men to talk about this stuff versus keep it to themselves or just miserably failing to play the game of love or dating or whatever you call it effectively.

Note that information is powerful but it's only potential. It's the application of the information that really changes the game. Do not just read this, do what you read. In doing so you will experience more meaningful relationships and ultimately find your true love.

I'm excited to hear of the stories as you go forth and make this information work. It's my hope that there will be less divorces, less broken homes, less heart broken women because we now had a conversation of what it takes to really succeed in dating with a purpose.

Thank you for giving me your attention and letting a regular man share some real regular stuff that come from real experiences. This has always been a dream of mine to write a book and that dream is what you're holding in your hands right now. Know that a new history can be made, whatever you know about dating can change. It's a gamble for sure, but there are some gambles where it's worth all the risk. Good look in your pursuit of finding that gamble.

ABOUT ANTHONY DRAYTON:

I've been the player and dealer at the table of dating. Over my years I've played numerous different roles as I've adapted to the women that I was dealing with. At times using the tricks of the trade to bluff people in order to win the table and other times as the dealer fixing games to win for the house. Consider this book in some way my gambler anonymous decree, with the game called dating.

Instagram: Tonydray605
Facebook: Anthony Drayton
Snapchat: TonyDray

Made in the USA
Middletown, DE
14 January 2020